Fact Finders®

GENETICS

HEREDITY

Mason Anders

raintree

a Capstone company — publishers for children

Raintree is an imprint of Capstone Global Library Limited, a company incorporated in England and Wales having its registered office at 264 Banbury Road, Oxford, OX2 7DY – Registered company number: 6695582

www.raintree.co.uk
myorders@raintree.co.uk

Edited by Nikki Potts
Designed by Philippa Jenkins
Original illustrations © Capstone Global Library Limited 2017
Picture research by Morgan Walters and Jo Miller
Production by Katy LaVigne
Originated by Capstone Global Library Limited
Printed and bound in China

ISBN 978-1-4747-4401-0
21 20 19 18 17
10 9 8 7 6 5 4 3 2 1

British Library Cataloguing in Publication Data
A full catalogue record for this book is available from the British Library.

Acknowledgements
We would like to thank the following for permission to reproduce photographs: Alamy: Photo Researchers, Inc, 16; Newscom: Monty Rakusen Cultura, 23, World History Archive, 14; Science Source, 17; Shutterstock: BigBigbb1, 27, Blamb, 24, Designua, 22 (bottom), Dianne McFadden, 8, Dieter Hawlan, 19, FotoRequest, 7, Future Vectors, 5, Grandpa, 15, gritsalak karalak, 28, joshya, 25, kentoh, cover (inset), 1, Odua Images, cover, Patrick Foto, 4, Piotr Marcinski, 11, PoohFotoz, 12, ruigsantos, 26, Sebastian Kaulitzki, 3, special for you, throughout, (background), Tatjana Romanova, 10, Ubrx, 21, Wuttichok Panichiwarapun, 20, youyuenyong budsawongkod, 9; SuperStock: Maximilian S/Michael Rosenfeld, 22 (top)

Every effort has been made to contact copyright holders of material reproduced in this book. Any omissions will be rectified in subsequent printings if notice is given to the publisher.

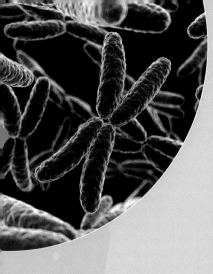

CONTENTS

CHAPTER 1

What is heredity?

Family members often look like each other. Perhaps you and your father share the same shaped nose. Maybe you are tall, like your mother. These and many other features are called **traits**. The sum of all your traits is your phenotype.

Traits such as eye colour and hair colour are inherited from parents.

trait a quality or characteristic that makes one person or animal different from another

Heredity is the passing of traits from parents to their offspring. We inherit traits from our parents. They inherited traits from their parents. Inherited traits are passed from one **generation** to the next through **genes**.

Genetics is the study of heredity, and genes are the basic units of heredity. Genes direct how living things develop, function and reproduce. A zebra's genes give it stripes. A bird's genes give it wings. Genes determine whether you have blue, green or brown eyes. Our genes give us fingers and everything else that makes us human. All together, the genes that produce the phenotype are the genotype. They are arranged into larger structures called **chromosomes**.

Each cell follows the instructions of its genes. They tell cells how to develop and what to do. All of the cells work together to make stripes, wings or fingers.

NATURAL SELECTION

Phenotypes are also influenced by environmental factors. Because of this, an individual's phenotype may change throughout life due to environmental changes.

Natural selection is how phenotypes and genotypes change within a population over a long period of time. The idea behind natural selection is that the individuals best suited to gain the most resources will be the ones best able to reproduce and pass on their genes.

Imagine an island with the same species of beetle. Some are red. Some are brown. The beetles are prey for a bird. The bird has an easier time spotting the red beetles. Therefore, the red beetles are more likely to be eaten and brown beetles will reproduce at a higher rate. Over time there are fewer and fewer red beetles. In time that trait dies out in favour of the more useful one, and only brown beetles will remain.

generation a group of people born around the same time

gene tiny unit of a cell that determines the characteristics that an offspring gets from his or her parents

chromosome thread-like structure in the nucleus that carries the genes

Passing genes to offspring

Reproduction is necessary for a species to survive. Genes are passed along when a plant or animal reproduces.

Many plants and animals pass genes to their offspring through sexual reproduction. Sex cells from each parent join together, and the two cells form a new individual. The female sex cell is an egg. The male sex cell is a sperm.

Most cells in a living thing are body cells. Your muscle cells are body cells. So are your skin and nerve cells. All of your body cells have two sets of chromosomes. Every human body cell has 23 pairs of chromosomes. That makes 46 chromosomes in all. One set in the pair comes from the father. The other set comes from the mother.

Eggs and sperm are different from other cells. They have half the number of chromosomes of body cells. Sex cells unite to make an offspring with a full set of 46 chromosomes. One of the chromosome pairs is special. These are the sex chromosomes. Females have two X chromosomes. Males have one X and one Y chromosome. The other chromosomes are called autosomes.

FACT

Sometimes a completely new variation appears in the genetic material of an offspring. These sudden changes are called mutations. Mutations can be harmful or useful.

An Eastern bluebird's specific colouring is determined by its genetic make-up.

CHAPTER 2

Dominant and recessive genes

Family members often resemble one another. But sometimes they look very different. A sister may be tall. A brother may be short. Your mother and father may have dark hair. Yours might be red.

The gene for red hair is recessive. A person needs to inherit two of these genes to have red hair.

These differences happen because each gene comes in different forms called **alleles**. The gene that determines hair colour has many alleles. One of the alleles could make your hair black. Another might give you brown or blonde hair.

You inherited two alleles for each gene. One came from your father, and one came from your mother. Gene alleles get mixed up during reproduction. They make every person unique. Often, a father and mother do not have the same type of alleles. Their child gets a mixture of alleles. Babies inherit alleles for every kind of trait.

Some alleles are **dominant**. Other alleles are **recessive**. A child may inherit dominant or recessive alleles. If the child inherits two dominant alleles, the dominant trait will show up. If the child inherits two recessive alleles, the recessive trait will emerge. What if the child inherits one dominant allele and one recessive allele? The dominant trait wins out.

Dominant and recessive genes are found in all animals. The black colour gene in cats is dominant. A black cat has either one or two genes for black colouring.

allele one of two genes in a pair contributed by a parent

dominant the form of a gene most likely to produce a trait in offspring

recessive the form of a gene most likely to stay hidden

Earlobes are a good example of dominant and recessive genes. If earlobes hang free from the side of your head, they are unattached. If they connect to the side of your head, they are attached. The allele for unattached earlobes is dominant. The allele for attached earlobes is recessive.

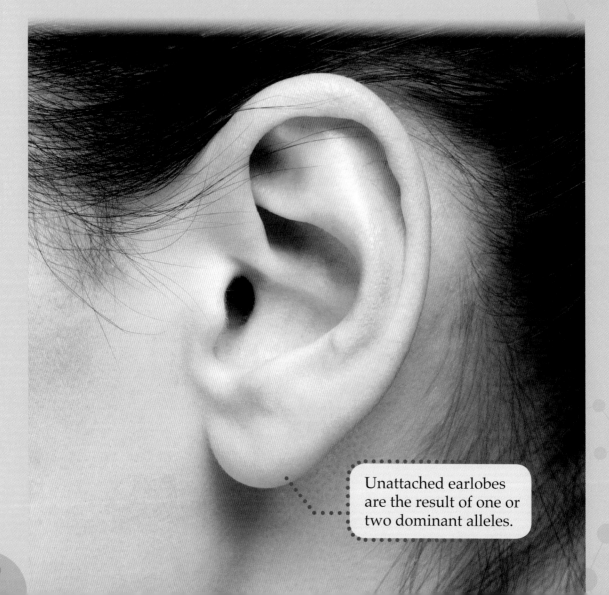

Unattached earlobes are the result of one or two dominant alleles.

If your mother has attached earlobes, she has two recessive earlobe alleles. If your father has unattached earlobes, he may have one dominant and one recessive allele, or he may have two dominant alleles.

What kind of earlobes do you have? If you have attached earlobes, each of your parents gave you two recessive alleles. If you have unattached earlobes, you have one or two dominant alleles.

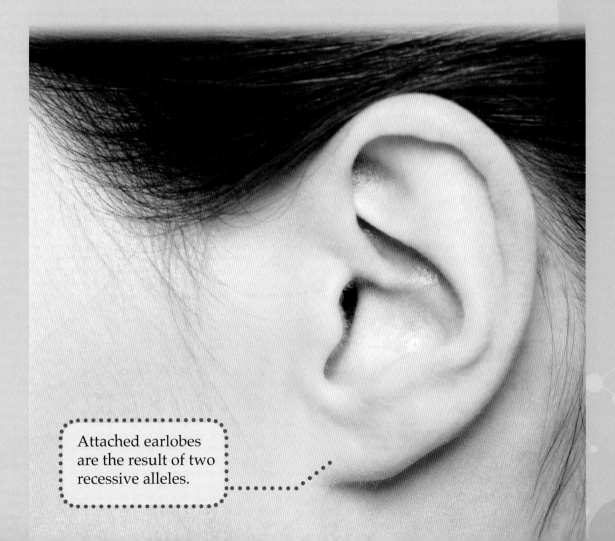

Attached earlobes are the result of two recessive alleles.

CHAPTER 3

Punnett Squares and probability

Reginald Punnett (1875–1967) was a British scientist. He developed an easy way to figure out allele combinations. His method is called the Punnett Square. It shows the chances that a specific trait will appear.

The Punnett Squares on the next page are for attached or unattached earlobes. Along the side are the father's genes. On the top are the mother's genes. The upper case letter U is a dominant allele. The lower case letter u is a recessive gene. Each square stands for a possible combination of alleles.

Reginald Punnett attended Cambridge University in the United Kingdom and became its first professor of genetics in 1912.

This Punnett Square tells us that the child of these parents will have a 50 per cent chance of having attached earlobes. There is a 50 per cent chance of having unattached earlobes.

	Mother's allele u	Mother's allele u
Father's allele U	Uu	Uu
Father's allele u	uu	uu

What if each parent has one dominant gene and one recessive gene for attached earlobes? The Punnett Square would look like this:

	Mother's allele U	Mother's allele u
Father's allele U	UU	Uu
Father's allele u	Uu	uu

The child of these parents would have a 75 per cent chance of having unattached earlobes.

CHAPTER 4

Mendel's peas

Gregor Mendel (1822–1884) was the first person to discover the laws of heredity. Before Mendel, people thought that the traits of an offspring were always a blend of the parents' traits. They believed that if a tall person and a short person had a baby, the child would be of medium height.

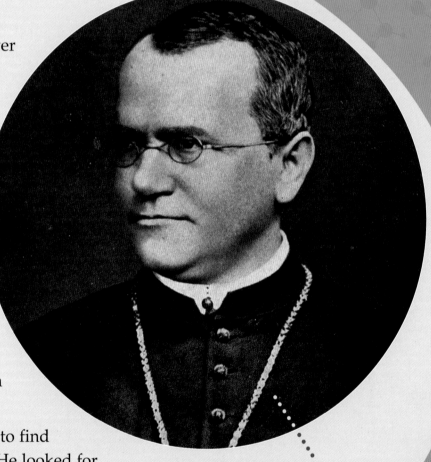

Gregor Mendel

Mendel wanted to find out if this was true. He looked for a simple system to study. He decided to **breed** strains of pea plants.

breed to keep animals or plants under controlled conditions so they produce more and better quality offspring

A Q-tip is used to hand-pollinate a cucumber blossom.

ARTIFICIAL SELECTION

Artificial selection is a process by which humans mould an organism's evolution. Instead of nature guiding the process, people select the traits of an organism that are passed on to offspring.

Artificial selection, also called selective breeding, has been around for a long time.

People learned how to grow the seeds of plants they once gathered in the wild. At the end of the growing season, they harvested crops and collected new seeds.

The plants of some seeds produced more grain than others. People saved those seeds and used them to plant the next crop. Other seeds produced plants that could resist disease. People saved and planted these seeds too. They planted different varieties of seeds together. Some of these new plants gave a lot of grain and resisted disease.

Flowering plants like peas need two parents. They can only make seeds when **pollen** from the flower of one plant is carried to the flower of another. In nature, bees, other insects or wind do the job. But humans can do it too. Mendel moved the pollen from the flowers of tall peas to the flowers of short peas.

pollen a powder made by flowers to help them create new seeds

What Mendel found was a surprise. The traits of the two parents did not just blend together to make pea plants of medium height. All of the new plants were tall, even though one of the parents was short.

Mendel found offspring do not necessarily have an even mix of parents' traits.

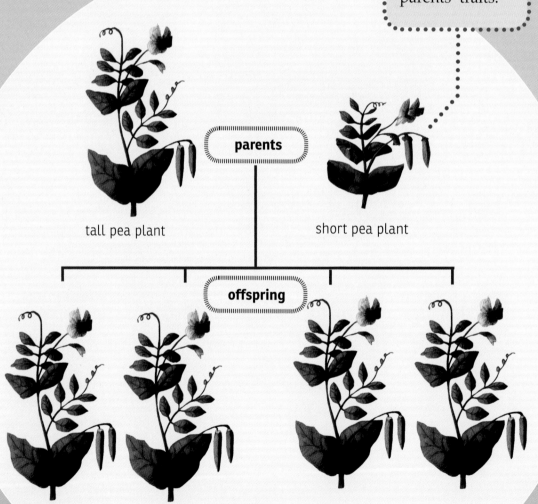

parents

tall pea plant

short pea plant

offspring

tall pea plants

Mendel concluded that traits are determined by "factors" passed on to the offspring. An individual inherits a pair of factors for each trait, one from each parent. One factor is dominant. The other factor is recessive. A trait may not show up in an individual, but it can be passed on to the next generation. We now know that these so-called factors are genes.

Mendel bred peas for seven years. During that time he counted 300,000 peas. The scientist published his findings in 1866, but no one paid attention to his paper. In 1900 scientists rediscovered Mendel's work. The science of genetics was born.

Mendel's discovery of genetics led to the study of heredity in other species, such as *Primula sinesis*.

CHAPTER 5

Modes of inheritance

Mendel was lucky when he chose to study peas. Each trait he studied had just two alleles. One was completely dominant. The other was completely recessive. Things are not always so simple in living things. Geneticists now know that there are other forms of inheritance.

Codominance

Some alleles are equally dominant. We say they are codominant. In this case, both traits appear in the offspring. For example, cattle with two alleles for red hair colour are all red. Cattle with two alleles for white hair colour are all white. The offspring of a red cow and a white bull will produce a roan calf. It has both red and white hairs.

FACT

The blood type AB is an example of codominance. The A and B alleles received from each parent are equally dominant.

The red and white genes of roan calves are equally dominant – codominant. Both colours are visible.

Incomplete dominance

Some alleles show incomplete dominance. The offspring shows a blend of both traits.

A good example is flower colour. A red snapdragon has two dominant alleles for red flowers. We call them RR. A white snapdragon has two recessive alleles for white flowers. They are rr. The red alleles are incompletely dominant over the white alleles. A cross between a red and a white snapdragon results in pink flowers. They all have the genotype Rr.

Something interesting happens when two pink flowers produce more flowers. Each parent flower has the same genotype, which is Rr.

Half of the offspring will be pink. One quarter will be red. One quarter will be white.

Pink snapdragons are the result of incomplete dominance of the red allele over the white allele.

Complex forms of heredity

Some traits are affected by more than one gene. Eye colour and skin colour are examples of traits that are affected by several genes.

Eye colour is determined by which dominant and recessive alleles you receive from your parents.

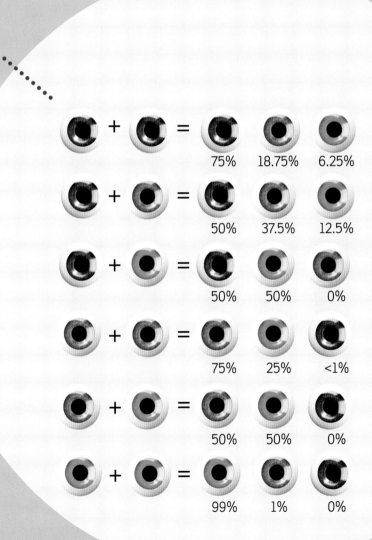

CHAPTER 6

Mapping our genes

Genetic scientists are trying to discover where every gene is on each human chromosome. They want to understand what each gene does. This knowledge will help doctors diagnose genetic diseases. It will help researchers to find cures for diseases that are caused by **defective** genes. Scientists have identified more than 4,000 diseases that result from defective gene alleles.

Geneticists analyze the base sequencing of genes to try and diagnose genetic diseases.

chromosome

DNA strand

Genes are the sections that make up DNA strands. DNA is packaged into chromosomes.

defective less valuable or useful because of a fault or weakness

The technique for finding genes is called **gene mapping**. Scientists can study inheritance patterns in a family. This helps them identify the regions of chromosomes that carry certain gene alleles.

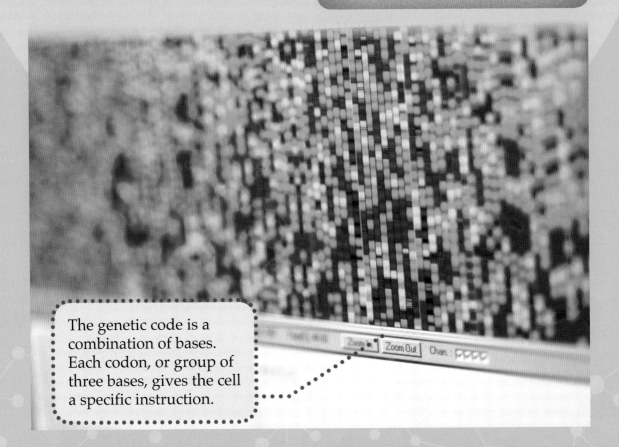

The genetic code is a combination of bases. Each codon, or group of three bases, gives the cell a specific instruction.

gene mapping the process of determining the relative positions of, and distances between, genes on a chromosome

Huntington's disease kills off nerve cells in the brain. It is a deadly disorder. Scientists have found the allele for the gene that causes Huntington's disease. Couples with a family history of the disease can be tested to determine whether they carry the allele. They can use that information to decide whether they want to have children.

Huntington's disease causes enlarged parts of the brain and degeneration, or decaying, of nerve cells. The disease can affect judgment, memory and other mental functions.

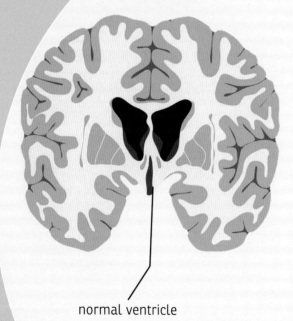

normal brain

normal ventricle

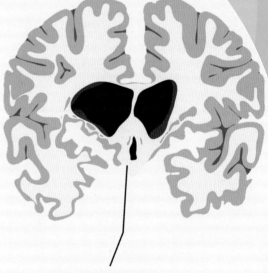

brain with Huntington's disease

enlarged ventricle

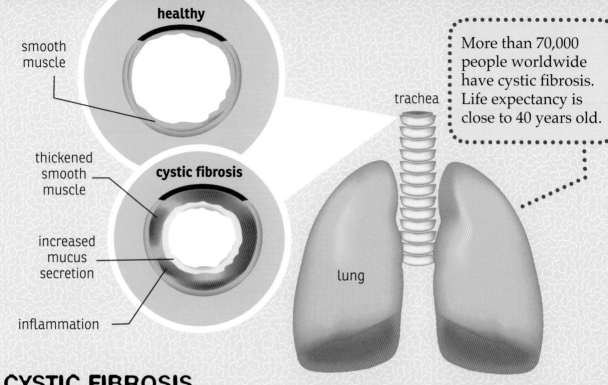

healthy

smooth muscle

thickened smooth muscle

increased mucus secretion

inflammation

cystic fibrosis

trachea

lung

More than 70,000 people worldwide have cystic fibrosis. Life expectancy is close to 40 years old.

CYSTIC FIBROSIS

Cystic fibrosis is a genetic disease caused by a defective gene. Cystic fibrosis affects the lungs, pancreas and other organs. In the lungs, mucus clogs up the airways, trapping bacteria. This can cause infections, lung damage and eventually respiratory failure. In the pancreas, the excess mucus prevents enzymes from being released. These digestive enzymes aid in breaking down food and absorbing nutrients.

People with cystic fibrosis have inherited the defective gene from both parents. When both parents pass on their defective gene, the child has a 25 per cent chance of having cystic fibrosis. People with one only one defective gene are carriers, but they do not have the disease.

Cystic fibrosis affects each person differently. However, treatments are often similar. Airways need to be cleared daily to get rid of the buildup of mucus. Inflatable vests that vibrate are often used. **Nebulizers** help open up airways. **Enzymes** are also taken daily with each meal to help the body absorb nutrients.

nebulizer a device that converts medicine into a fine spray to be breathed in

enzyme a protein that helps break down food

CHAPTER 7

Sex-linked traits

Most often, alleles appear on chromosomes that are not sex chromosomes. They affect both males and females. But some alleles are found on sex chromosomes. The traits they code are linked to the individual's sex. The human X chromosome is much larger than the Y chromosome. It contains many more genes. As a result, there are many more X-linked traits than Y-linked traits.

Male pattern baldness is a sex-linked trait that can come from either the mother or father.

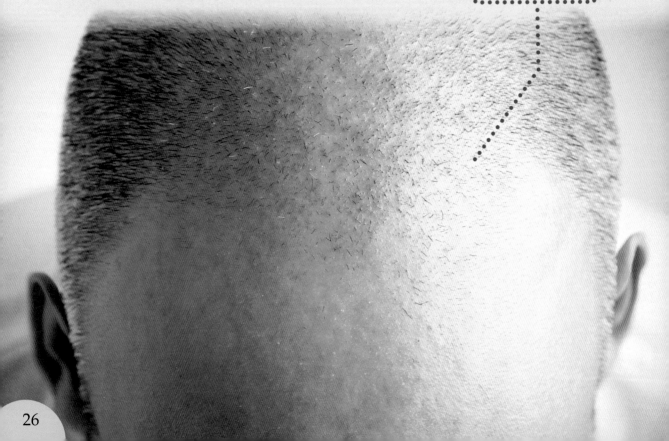

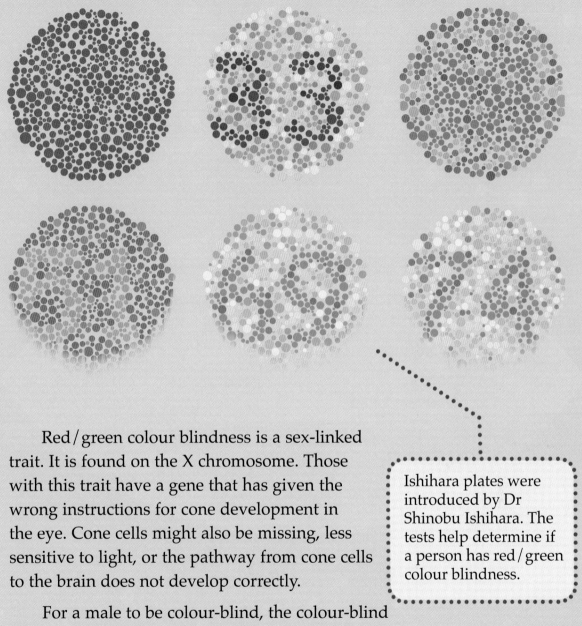

Red/green colour blindness is a sex-linked trait. It is found on the X chromosome. Those with this trait have a gene that has given the wrong instructions for cone development in the eye. Cone cells might also be missing, less sensitive to light, or the pathway from cone cells to the brain does not develop correctly.

For a male to be colour-blind, the colour-blind gene needs to show on his single X chromosome. For a female to be colour-blind, the gene must be present on both of her X chromosomes.

Ishihara plates were introduced by Dr Shinobu Ishihara. The tests help determine if a person has red/green colour blindness.

Haemophilia is a disorder in which blood cannot clot properly. It is a sex-linked trait. Clotting helps bleeding stop after a cut. A person with haemophilia can bleed too much after an injury.

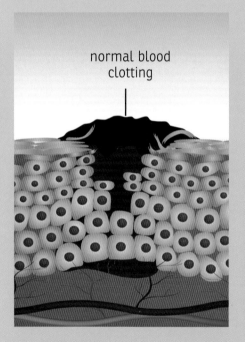

normal blood clotting

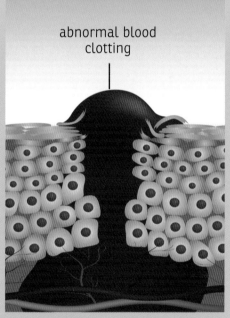

abnormal blood clotting

The gene for a **protein** that helps blood clot is on the X chromosome. Women have two X chromosomes. Most of the time at least one has the normal blood-clotting gene. A woman with one defective gene and one normal gene is a carrier. She will not have the disease, but she can pass the gene to her offspring.

protein chemical made by plant and animal cells to carry out various functions

If she passes the X chromosome with the defective gene to a son, he will have the disease. He has only one copy of the gene. Girls can only inherit haemophilia if the genes on both of her X chromosomes are defective.

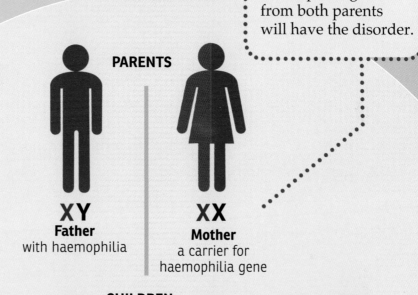

A daughter that has inherited the haemophilia gene from both parents will have the disorder.

PARENTS

XY
Father
with haemophilia

XX
Mother
a carrier for
haemophilia gene

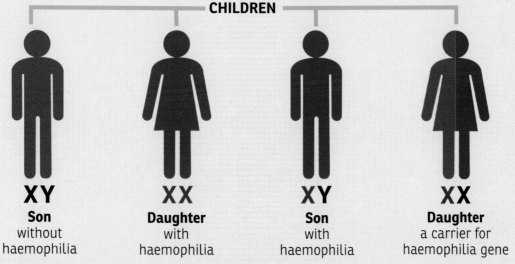

CHILDREN

XY
Son
without
haemophilia

XX
Daughter
with
haemophilia

XY
Son
with
haemophilia

XX
Daughter
a carrier for
haemophilia gene

Glossary

allele one of two genes in a pair contributed by a parent

breed to keep animals or plants under controlled conditions so they produce more and better quality offspring

chromosome thread-like structure in the nucleus that carries the genes

defective less valuable or useful because of a fault or weakness

dominant the form of a gene most likely to produce a trait in offspring

enzyme a protein that helps break down food

gene tiny unit of a cell that determines the characteristics that an offspring gets from his or her parents

gene mapping the process of determining the relative positions of, and distances between, genes on a chromosome

generation a group of people born around the same time

nebulizer a device that converts medicine into a fine spray to be breathed in

pollen a powder made by flowers to help them create new seeds

protein chemical made by plant and animal cells to carry out various functions

recessive the form of a gene most likely to stay hidden

trait a quality or characteristic that makes one person or animal different from another

Find out more

Inheritance of Traits: Why Is My Dog Bigger Than Your Dog? (Show Me Science), Jen Green (Raintree, 2014)

Introduction to Genes and DNA, Anna Claybourne (Usborne Publishing, 2015)

The Story of You, Anna Claybourne (Wayland, 2016)

Websites

www.bbc.co.uk/schools/gcsebitesize/science/ocr_gateway/ understanding_organisms/variation_inheritancerev5.shtml
This BBC website has information about inherited disorders including colour blindness and cystic fibrosis.

www.ducksters.com/science/biology/mendel_and_ inheritance.php
Visit this website for more information about Gregor Mendel and his studies of heredity.

www.sciencemuseum.org.uk/whoami/findoutmore/ yourgenes
Visit the Science Museum website to find out about genes, how they work and what causes genetic disorders.

Comprehension questions

- How are genes related to inherited traits?

- Genes come in different forms – alleles. Alleles can be either dominant or recessive. What do these terms mean?

- Do you have attached or unattached earlobes? What types of alleles did your parents give you for you to have this trait?

Index